Simple Manners and
Modern Etiquette

HOW NOT
TO BE A
JERK

By M.K. Dougherty/Mueller

How Not to Be a Jerk Simple Manners and Modern Etiquette 2016 by
M.K. Dougherty/Mueller

Bootstrap Publishing Institute
480-560-4933 Arizona
585-342-0795 New York
mkd@bootstrappublising.net
www.Bootstrappublishing.net

First edition
ISBN 1517001382
Library of Congress Catalog Number

Mary K Dougherty at RocCity Book Publishing is Professional,
supportive and individualized guidance for writing, marketing or
publishing your book! We can now make virtual writer author
consultations via SKYPE! To arrange a free 20-minute talk and/or
question-and-answer session for your class, please email
publisher@bootstrappublishing.net

Manufacturing in the United States of America

*"Good manners will open doors that the best
education cannot."*
~Clarence Thomas

Manners and will improve your relationships with people immeasurably when you show them that you care about them!

Manners are kindness.

Manners are Karma.

This book is for you if.......
Someone tells you **"you have no manners. "**

When you don't know why or how you are pissing off others.

Why you have lost friends and don't know why.

You're are not getting promoted at work.

You're not making the money you need and want.

When others stop being generous to you.

Can't get a date.

You view the world as a hard place to live.

When you never did learn to be kind and considerate of others.

When you have zilch for Class.
Or need a brushing up on it.

Or you are just a jerk...............
Stop blaming others and get what you want out of life. **_Read this book._**

BASIC MANNERS

Don't point - it's rude

Don't talk with your mouth full, you may spit some of it out!

Don't shout - Keep your voice down

Don't interrupt - it's selfish and ill-mannered

Open doors for the elderly and for women

Hold doors open for whoever is following you in (or out) - don't let it slam in their face

Use please and thank you

Don't talk behind other's backs

Turn away from people, food and the phone
when you cough or sneeze

Show respect for those older and wiser than
yourself

That would be me.

Wash your hands after going to the restroom.

If you bump into someone, say excuse me.

Don't reach across someone's face.

Don't stay behind the crosswalk when you are making a left turn and thus prevent anyone else behind you from turning.

Don't let your kids act like wild monkeys in a restaurant.

Keep your elbows off of the table while eating;

Don't touch someone's belly when she's pregnant–or even when she isn't.

Don't leave cupboard doors and drawers open— someone can get hurt.

People don't care how much you know;
Until they know how much you care.

BASIC PROFESSIONAL ETIQUETTE RULES:

- Maintain a professional image when decorating your office or cubicle.
- When socializing with your coworkers, don't do anything you don't want mentioned at the office later.
- Never interrupt conversations.
- If you must eat at your desk, and you work in a cubicle, avoid foods with strong odors.
- Remove papers from the copier, fax machine, and scanner after you are finished with the task.
- Shake hands when appropriate.
- Praise others for a job well done.
- Never take credit for other people's work.
- Always arrive on time.
- Dress appropriately for your office environment.
- Don't touch other people's personal belongings.
- Observe proper etiquette with regard to personal space.

- Participate in office donations, but don't make an issue of how much or how little you give.
- Keep office correspondence brief and avoid interjecting personal opinions unless it is necessary.
- Be friendly to clients, visitors, and guests. Offer them a comfortable seat if they have to wait.
- Use your indoor voice and avoid yelling.
- If someone else is angry, refuse to join in an argument rant.
- Stop gossiping Now.

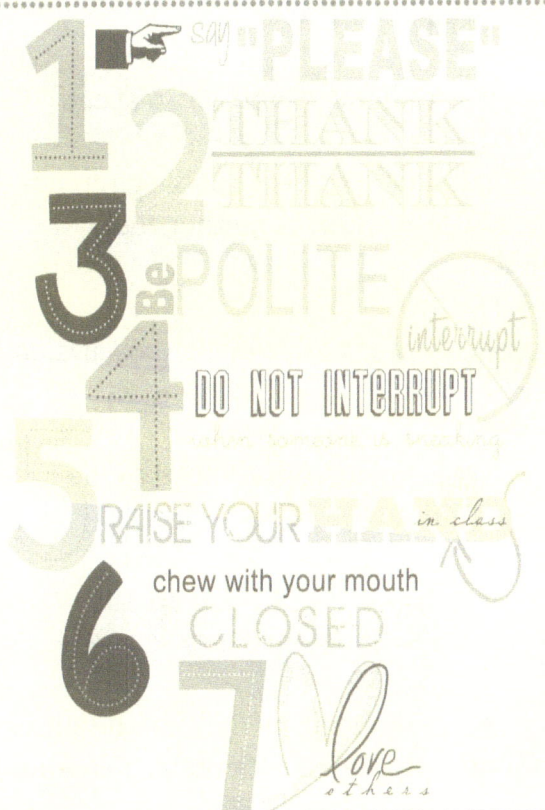

MANNERS

1 say "PLEASE"

2 THANK

THANK

3 Be POLITE

4 DO NOT INTERRUPT

interrupt

5 RAISE YOUR HAND in class

6 chew with your mouth CLOSED

7 love others

MORE OFFICE MANNERS

is about conducting yourself politely and courteously in the office or workplace

Always act with honesty and self-respect

Chewing gum and popping bubble gum in the presence of co-workers is neither cool nor dignified

No exposed midriff to display tattoos and body piercing.

Be neat, clean and as conservative as the business requires you to be

First impressions are vital! You are the representative/s of the business

We are put off by smelly people. So, be sure to shower regularly and use a suitable deodorant

Do not cough or sneeze in anyone's direction. Use a tissue, if possible, to contain the germs and then say "Excuse me"

The essence of good manners and etiquette is to be respectful and courteous at all times and with everybody

Therefore, treat your co-workers, cleaners, maintenance people and others with respect and courtesy

Keep your interruptions of others to a minimum and always apologize if your intrusion is an interruption of a discussion, someone's concentration or other activity

Show respect for each other's workspace. Knock before entering

Show appreciation for the slightest courtesies extended to you

Be helpful and co-operative with each other

Brush up on your computer skills so that you can help others

You will find help from some of the sponsors listed at the top or right side of this page. Check them out as well

Speak clearly

Say, "Please; Thank you; you're welcome", as part of your everyday courtesy

Be discreet and compassionate in your criticism of a co-worker

Don't gossip about any co-worker's private life

Do not try to sell things to your colleagues

Don't hover around while waiting for a co-worker to get off the phone. Leave a note for them to call you or return later

It's not a good idea to take your iPod to your office. It hinders communication

Avoid sexist comments about a co-worker's dress or appearance

Surveys show that the office know-it-all proved to be the biggest gripe amongst co-workers. Don't be a know-all

Take responsibility for your mistakes, apologize and go about correcting the mistakes

Apologize if you are clearly in the wrong. If in doubt, apologize anyway. It's no big deal

Never blame someone else if it is your mistake

If your boss criticizes your work, enquire about what precisely is wrong with it. Consider the comments, discuss them amiably if you disagree with the comments but defer to the boss's opinion if he/she is adamant

The boss always gets the benefit of the doubt. Don't argue with the boss (however, there are standards of etiquette for employers too.

Make new employees feel welcome and comfortable around you. Don't be a busy-body

Office etiquette means being thoughtful when interacting with your peers

Keep your work area tidy. Try not to be messy

Show consideration for other people's feelings

If there is conflict, do not get personal in your remarks

It is extremely rude to arrive late for a meeting

It is ruder still to not attend at all. Having a good excuse does not exonerate you

Do not dominate the meeting. All communication must take place through the chairperson

Pay attention to the proceedings quietly. Don't shuffle your papers

Do not leave the meeting until it is closed by the chairperson

Never be petty or small minded in your behavior

Always be particularly respectful to those older than yourself even if they are junior to you in position

Your elders are generally more mature in judgement and life's experiences and this deserves your respect even in the workplace

Practice good manners and office etiquette at every opportunity; even in the toilet

1. **Texting** "I'm running 10 minutes late" is not as acceptable as making the effort to be on time.

2. If you can't attend an event that you're formally invited to, don't think that not RSVP'ing is the same as declining. And don't RSVP at the last minute for an event that involves real planning by the host.

3. Show some decency around the office refrigerator: If you didn't put the food in, don't eat it. And take your leftovers home or throw them out before they morph into some radioactive nightmare.

4. **Don't bellow on your cell phone. Just because you can't hear the other person well doesn't mean the other person can't hear you well.**

5. Turn off the phone at a dinner party, and be in the moment. You're annoying at least one person who thinks you have no social skills. At bare minimum, turn off the ringer so you can text and conspire in relative stealth.

6. Remember that if you feel a need to respond immediately to every incoming text, you'll lose more in the eyes of the person who's in front of you than you'll gain from the unseen people who are benefiting from your efficiency.

7. When you get to the front of the line at Starbucks SBUX -0.05%, don't tell the barista to wait while you wrap up your phone discussion. The barista hates you, and so does everyone behind you. They are hoping the barista spits in your latte.

8. If you come late to an exercise class, don't think you're entitled to barge your way to your favorite spot in the front. And don't block others from weight racks or other equipment—just step back three feet and make everyone happy.

9. Keep personal conversations and arguments off social networking sites. The dramatic airing of grievances is best done through SMS.

10. Moderate your use of cameras and video at events. Enjoy your time with colleagues, friends and family in the present and preserve only a memento for the future, rather than recording the entire thing to "relive" later in some "free" time that you'll never actually have.

11. Remember how easily e-gossip can be forwarded along to the wrong person.

12. Just because you're wearing headphones doesn't mean you can tune out from social courtesies. For example, if you accidentally cross someone's personal space, apologize graciously.

13. Don't lend someone a book or item unless they specifically ask for it. They're probably too busy to ever get around to it. They'll feel guilty about that, and you'll be annoyed that they didn't appreciate it or even get around to returning it.

14. Don't RSVP for an event, then not show. Now you're not just being rude, but you're costing the host money, and you've probably kept a lonely soul from being invited as a backup.

15. Don't be the first or second person to talk on your cell phone in a public space (like a bus or train). If everyone's doing it, you're allowed some slack here.

16. Don't show up at a party empty-handed, unless you've been instructed to — and sometimes not even then. Bring wine or dessert or a plant.

17. Use your turn signal at least 50% more than you use your middle finger.

18. Don't make your dietary requirements everyone else's dilemma. As one friend reminds me, "People who can eat dairy don't just keep coconut oil-based butter around."

19. If your children are invited to a friend's house to play, they (and you) should also feel invited to help with the cleanup.

20. Don't break up with someone by text. And don't announce a death in the family by text. There are still times when phones or face-to-face are the best way to go.

21. Don't take photos for posting on the People of Walmart page.

22. Don't discuss sensitive personal issues on Facebook, especially if you've friended coworkers.

23. Your dog is cute, but he or she doesn't have a pass to go anywhere. "I'm a huge dog lover," says one colleague, "but don't assume its okay to bring along your dog to my house. I can barely stand what my own dogs do to my house ... I also

don't like people who bring their animals to Petco. Seriously, do you think your dog likes to shop? It's just you seeking attention. You probably don't even need anything at Petco... you're just there because you can bring your dog in, and you think it's cool to bring a dog out in public. Dogs don't shop. They would rather be sniffing the pee on that trashcan outside by the front door than walking on slippery retail flooring."

24. Double-check that your headphones are plugged-in before streaming your favorite Spotify station.

25. Don't say, "I'm having a party. Bring your own food and drink." That's not a party.

26. If you've been invited to an event, be reluctant to ask for an upper ceiling on how many friends and relatives you can bring.

Olive, Brutus, wimpy ....

Me mum, me pops and everyone from the 50s

It could be your business.

NETIQUETTE EMAIL ETIQUETTE IS JUST

a small part of Netiquette - no, that's not a typo! Netiquette is Internet Etiquette for all aspects of the internet, including e-mailing.

The most important and most used and abused is the e-mailing part of the net. Here are some rules to follow for forwarding E-mails. These rules are for those who are being truly considerate and thoughtful.

E-mail Etiquette
Rule 1. Don't forward anything without editing out all the forwarding >>>>>, other e-mail addresses, headers, and commentary from all the other forwarders.

People really don't want to look amongst all the gobble-gook to see what it is you thought was worth forwarding. If you must forward, only forward the actual 'guts' or content of the e-mail that you are of the opinion is valuable.

E-mail Etiquette
Rule 2. If you cannot take the time to write a personal comment at the top of your forwarded e-mail to the person you are sending to – then you shouldn't forward it at all.

E-mail Etiquette
Rule 3. Think carefully about if the e-mail you are forwarding will be of value (accurate information - check for hoaxes at Snopes.com), will it be appreciated (is it something the recipient is interested in or needs), if it is humorous (do they have the same sense of humor as you do).

If you cannot think of why the person you are forwarding to would like to receive the e-mail - then simply don't forward it.

E-mail Etiquette
Rule 4. It should go without saying that forwarding of e-mail chain letters; regardless how noble the topic may seem, virus warnings or anything that says 'forward to everyone you know', simply should not be forwarded because in most cases it is plain old garbage.

Remember, e-mail is only e-mail; it does not have any magical powers that can bring you bad luck or whatever else the chain letter threatens. By the same token it cannot bring you fame and fortune as they promise.

If you must forward an e-mail to more than one person, put your e-mail address in the To: field and all the others you are sending to in the Bcc: field to protect their e-mail address from being published to those they do not know.

This is a serious privacy issue! Do not perpetuate a breach of privacy started by other forwarders who included their contact's addresses in the To: or Cc: field by continuing to forward those visible addresses to your contacts.

Remove any e-mail addresses in the body of the e-mail that have been forwarded by those who disregard the privacy of their friends and associates.

Keep in mind that if you are forwarding a private e-mail that was sent to you, you must get the sender's permission to forward it on to others (or to post it publicly).

E-mails are copyright protected by their authors. Not only that, common courtesy dictates that you should ask the author first if the e-mail sent for your eyes only can be forwarded to strangers or others for which it was not originally intended.

Use the Subject field to enter a clear concise indication of what the e-mail is about. This is a very useful field and can be helpful to the recipient if used judiciously, so make it informative.

Type in capitals only if you mean to SHOUT. Now, it is ill-mannered to shout, so, type in lower case and remember your punctuation.

You do not want to give the impression of sloppiness. Save multi-colored text for love letters and kindergarten kids to express their creativity.

It is alright to intersperse your replies between a whole bunches of questions; just be sure to reply in a different colored text so that your replies stand out.

It would help to start the reply with the customary greeting and then refer the recipient to the answers written below each question.

Keep your attachments to less than one MB (if possible). It will transmit faster and avoid 'time-outs."

With all the above "rules" to consider would it be more friendly, personal and enjoyable to simply telephone them?

If one cannot make these extra efforts, then you really have no excuse for feeling hurt when asked to stop sending this unwanted mail.

If you are asked to stop forwarding, don't get mad; just realize the person on the other side is not interested or too busy to have to cope with a whole bunch of unwanted e-mail.

Also, they have every right to make that request.

At the end of the day, when it comes to receiving unwanted forwarded e-mails, if you fear hurting someone's feelings by asking them to stop forwarding you e-mails, just keep in mind they probably meant well, they were thinking of you and were trying to make a point .....

Business E-mails

Businesses are being swamped with email to such an extent that productivity is being affected.

A lot can be done to avoid propagating email stress and corporate spam by observing the following points:

- avoid sending an email unless it is absolutely necessary

- avoid sending copies or forwarding emails to persons not directly involved in the subject matter

- if you must forward an email, delete the parts that are irrelevant to the recipient

- think carefully before you decide to click "reply to all"

- do not request a delivery receipt or that the email has been read unless such information is vital

- if you reply just to say "thanks" you are contributing to corporate spam. It's courteous, but is it necessary?

- use the Subject field to concisely and accurately describe the contents

- avoid ambiguity to stop a further exchange of emails seeking clarification

- keep the contents clear and to the point

- does your email really require a reply? If not just end with NRN (no reply necessary) of aggravation in our society.

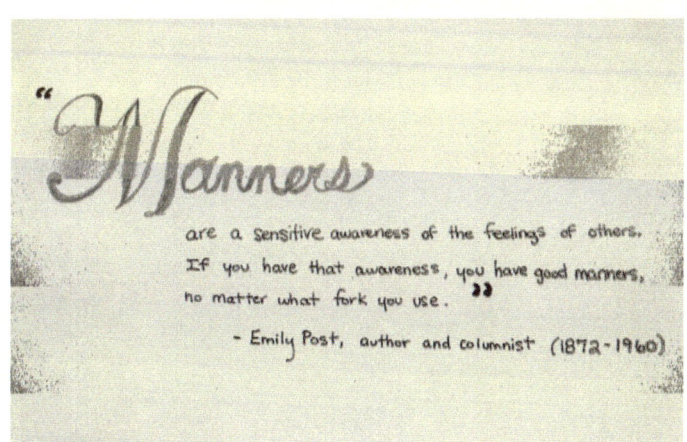

"Manners

are a sensitive awareness of the feelings of others. If you have that awareness, you have good manners, no matter what fork you use. "

- Emily Post, author and columnist (1872-1960)

Friends and good manners will carry you where money won't go."
~Margaret Walker

EMPLOYER ETIQUETTE

Is How You Conduct Yourself in Your Capacity As An Employer To Your Employees

Be respectful to your employees. Do not play favourites with any of them or you will quickly lose the respect of the rest of them

If an employee disagrees with you, hear them out. Give them your full attention. You may learn something useful from them. You will certainly get a different perspective on the subject.

This is an excellent opportunity to test your skill at handling the disagreement with tact and sensitivity. Never be dismissive or invalidate your employee's point of view. Do not trivialise their opinion

Get to know your employees; remember what they tell you about themselves. Keep notes to help your memory if necessary

Be sure to know their names

Respect what is told to you in confidence

Introduce new employees to their co-workers and have proper indoctrination procedures in place to make them feel welcome and useful from the start

Tell them what you expect of them

Let them get on with it

Help them when they need it

Tell them how they are doing

Reward and encourage them

Give them credit for their contribution

Do not take them for granted

Don't 'snooper vise' (snooping supervision)

Deal with employee grievances promptly and fairly. Do NOT trivialize them

Even though you are the boss, good etiquette requires that you keep your interruptions to a minimum and always apologize if your intrusion is an interruption to their concentration, a discussion or other activity

Dress smartly as an example to your employees

People don't care how much you know;
Until they know how much you care.

That may seem like a lot, and to some it may
seem like an tense way to live. But just
remember the basic success principle underlying
all manners: Think about other people's feelings
first because it's still not all about you.

DATING ETIQUETTE

comes naturally to people who already have good manners and show consideration for others at all times

It is second nature to them; they are not self-centered and are respected by people of either sex

When people date they usually share a common objective – they hope to win over the object of their affection

They therefore want to give a favorable impression of themselves

Hopefully, they will also bring out the best in their date

The fact that you have read this far indicates that you want to know how to behave properly on your date so that you can practice good dating etiquette; a good start!

The rules are basically the same for teens, the middle aged and seniors, first date or last date, girls or guys

Primary rule – girls and guys, treat your date with dignity and respect; this applies to online dating as well

Don't know what dignity and respect are? Read on to find out:

No swearing. Broaden your vocabulary beyond a few repetitive expletives

No drunkenness. Being stoned or wasted only gets a laugh from your mates at your expense

Act like a lady or gentleman. You will feel better for it

Be genuine. It must come from the heart

Be that way during your first date right until your last and see what a difference it will make to you, your date's and your life

Do not expect your prospect to be available for a date at short notice

Ask a few days in advance of the proposed date

Set a meeting time and if possible an ending time

If the person cannot or will not be available for a date at the second request – they are not interested
Don't push the issue. Move on

Guys usually initiate the first date or two (it is OK for the girl to initiate it if they are already good friends) after that either may do so

Whoever initiates it – plan to have at least one alternative place to go to or of what to do

Give the other person time to think about it and perhaps come up with other options

Discuss it with dignity. This is a good opportunity to agree on who pays for what?

Guys, be prepared to pay for the date (especially the first one)

Subsequent ones can be worked out in due course when you know a bit more about each other

Never spring it on her to 'cough up'

If you pay, understand that there must be no strings attached

Girls, be considerate - offer to pay half OR to buy the drinks or something to show that you are not a freeloader. It'll blow the socks off them!!

Then there can be no strings attached and you can maintain your independence

But don't sweat the issue - you could talk about it on the way to the venue so that you are prepared

You could offer to cook a meal or bring a picnic basket to the next date if there is the possibility of a follow up date

Be prepared ahead of time to have a few topics for light hearted conversation; nothing too controversial

No strong opinions please

Remember that the objective of a date is generally to assess the potential of coming together to be a couple in a close permanent relationship in so far as permanency goes
Never stand up your date

Postpone rather than cancel

Do not just fail to show up. That would be despicable

Be on time. It shows respect for your date's time. If you are running late ring and give a new ETA

Dress appropriately for the occasion. Clean hair, clothes and person. Lightly perfumed or with deodorizer/after shave

Guys – open, hold open and close doors for your date (even if she is driving)

It shows that you are prepared to go out of your way to be courteous to her

Girls - let him, but don't expect it

Either way, be gracious about it; smile or thank him

This is not the time to push your liberated female views

Some other time...maybe

Girls usually precede guys in the theatre, church, movies, to the table at a restaurant and most other places and guys help her to be seated - this is sophisticated dating etiquette

Guys on the other hand lead the way through crowds and traffic

On sidewalks, guys should walk nearest the street to 'protect' the girl - you get the idea

Complement each other

Neither one of you is perfect, there has to be something to compliment with sincerity

Look for it. Hair; clothes; smile; car; jewelry?

If you can't find something to compliment, why are you dating this person?

Blind date? Practice being gracious right to the end

Next time start with a cup of coffee first – just to test the water

Do not abandon your date at the venue

Be close and attentive or it may become your last date with that person

Being attentive to your date does not mean totally excluding all others in the group or at the party

Be pleasant to your date

Talking down to your date or being patronizing is not good etiquette

Remember your manners. Say – please, thank you, after you, you're welcome, etc

Acknowledge each other's' courtesies with a smile and/or 'thank you'

Show a keen interest in your date

Make frequent eye contact (do not leer)

Use their name – frequently. To them it is the sweetest word in any language

Never feign affection. This is cruel and deceitful and could lead to problems

If this is a first date enquire delicately to elicit information about likes and dislikes; values and expectations; interests, dreams and aspirations

At each subsequent date widen the field of your enquiry in a casual conversational manner while also imparting more information about yourself

Avoid bragging and talking too much about anything, especially yourself

Turn the conversation around to get your date's views and contribution to the subject

Keep the conversation light and try to have fun together

Use humor, but don't overdo it

Keep it clean

Don't lie to your date

Ask before you smoke

Non-smokers sometimes cannot abide smoker's breath or are allergic to cigarette smoke

Definitely don't smoke during the meal

It is bad etiquette to enforce your own rights over the comfort of others. Don't do it

Do not have unreasonable expectations of your date

Remember – dignity and respect

Do what is expected of you and not what you want to do

Do not force intimacy. If it happens it happens

If not it's probably too soon

Avoid sharing confidences. It puts your date in an awkward position

Guys, see her to her door after the date

It's for her safety

A friendly hug in greeting or to say good bye may be OK or perhaps a kiss on the cheek. Play it by ear

If you promise to ring or contact your date again, you must do it – within a reasonable time frame or do not make the offer

Try no more than twice

It's OK to date others until you have clearly come to an understanding or are going steady

It is best to discuss your intentions with sensitivity and patience

Keep practicing good manners

Remember – dignity and respect

TIPPING ETIQUETTE can be quite a dilemma, especially when travelling overseas, but being prepared will prevent it from becoming an embarrassing situation.

T-I-P tip. 'To Insure Performance'. Some schools of thought believe that tipping should be done in advance – to insure (ensure) performance – especially if you want to impress someone.

Tipping in advance would take on a new challenge - how to know that you are tipping the right person (smile)?

Tipping can be tricky when it comes to takeout vendors.

Travel Tipping creates one of the biggest dilemmas facing the traveler in countries where tipping is the norm and expected.

Who to tip?

How much to tip?

How little to tip without appearing stingy?

Even when the tip is added to the bill as a service charge, a further tip is expected in many cases.

The service industry is notorious for this practice.

In the USA, Restaurant Tipping etiquette requires that a service provider be paid 15% to 20% of the bill rendered.

It would help to know that in the USA and Canada the internal revenue department assumes that a certain portion of a service person's wage is derived from tips and will add on that percentage and tax them on it.

Therefore, whether they receive a tip or not they will pay tax on it. So please be mindful of this and tip accordingly.

Also, if a tip is not given the person providing the service would be puzzled and wonder if their service has been inadequate ... especially if they have been very helpful and courteous.

Some European and Asian countries would be happy with a tip of 10% to 15%.

We are friendly and won't be hanging out for a tip!

Not much anyway (smile).

There are more than two hundred countries in this world of ours.

In some, inhabitants expect to be tipped, some discourage tipping and some would be surprised if tipped.

Ask your travel agent about what is expected in the places you visit.

So called 'Guides to Tipping' are so full of contradictions as to defy logic.

The practices must have evolved in various mystifying ways.

Assume that a tip is expected of you.

Use Common Sense to determine the amount.

This will always be a dilemma as you can see from our suggestions.

Just go with your 'gut feeling' when in doubt (smile).

Would it serve everyone better if tipping were to be replaced by raising the wages of the hired help and increasing the price of the tariff or commodity to cover it?

One could argue that this would lower the standard of service by diminishing the incentive to provide excellent service.

But the service may be lacking anyhow, even where tipping is the custom.

Tourists in particular are fair game to have money sucked directly out of their bank by hotels and sea cruise companies for gratuities and the like.

Out of their wallets by foreign governments for port charges, visas and various taxes.

And out of their pockets by all and sundry between the airport and their hotel room for tips.

Having said all the above, our research indicates that a Rule of Thumb for tipping etiquette does exist.

In countries where tipping is the custom, tip 10% of the commodity charge for ordinary service.

And up to 15% for superior service (20% in the USA and Canada).

Pay a dollar or two for minimal service provided and ten to fifteen dollars for exemplary service that has extricated you from a tricky situation.

So, be prepared.

Always carry a fist-full of dollar coins and notes (or local currency equivalent) to reward a service if you are within spitting distance of a hotel, restaurant or any place where someone may do something for you to make your life a little easier.

It goes without saying that when in a foreign country where tipping is expected, pay the dollar equivalent in the local currency.

That said, an increasing number of countries prefer US dollars to any other currency even their own.

• Tipping is not optional; only withhold tips in cases of outrageously bad service

• Airport & hotel porters $2 per bag, minimum per cart $5

• Bartenders 10-15% per round, minimum per drink $1

• Hotel maid's $2-4 per night, left under the card provided

• Restaurant servers 15-20%, unless a gratuity is already charged on the bill

• Taxi drivers 10-15%, rounded up to the next dollar

• Valet parking attendants At least $2 when handed back the keys

BASIC ETIQUETTE RULES FOR FAMILY MEMBERS:

- Respect each other's personal space.
- Respect each other's belongings.
- Don't interrupt when someone else is talking.
- Be on time for dinner.
- Say "Please" and "Thank you."
- Don't text or talk on your cell phone during a family meal.
- Chew with your mouth closed.
- Don't yell or call each other names.
- Pick up after yourself so someone else doesn't have to do it.

SOCIAL

- Give and receive compliments graciously.
- Refuse to gossip with and about friends. After all, if you share gossip with someone, that person will wonder what you are saying behind his or her back.
- Hold doors for anyone who seems to be struggling, including the elderly, physically challenged, and parents with young children.
- When you are invited to a party, don't show up empty-handed. Bring a host or hostess gift and something to share.
- If you are sick and contagious, let the other person know. It is generally best to postpone your plans and reschedule after you are feeling better, since it is rude to knowingly expose your friends to illness.
- Pay your share when you are with a friend or group. If you stiff your friends, they may not invite you again. This includes tipping.

BASIC SOCIAL MEDIA ETIQUETTE RULES:

- Never post anything on any forum that you wouldn't want the world to see.
- Avoid put-downs, regardless of how witty you think you are.
- Don't divulge too much information about yourself or your family. You can never be sure who all is watching. This includes posting dates you'll be out of town and when you are hiring a teenage sitter to watch your children. You must protect your family.
- Self-promotion is okay in limited amounts. There are others who need your attention, so take some time to respond to their posts and offer praise when needed.
- If you make a mistake on social media, own it. Apologize and avoid doing it again.
- Follow the rules of whatever social media you are using

FUNERAL ETIQUETTE

is vital; the last thing one wants to do is upset the bereaved by being ignorant or clumsy.

In this emotional time the family is dealing, not only with grief, but with other things such as funeral arrangements, wills, life insurance or the lack thereof, and the list goes on.

Probably the most hurtful act would be to keep silent because you just don't know what to do or say. Bookmark and Share

Usually when a family member, friend or acquaintance dies your first reaction is a feeling of 'what can I do to make them feel better?' or 'what can I do to help'.

Is there a specific custom that I should be aware of?

Your second reaction is a feeling of hesitancy. You ask yourself, 'Will I be intruding during their grief?'

Perhaps you feel your words would be totally inadequate to express your feelings of empathy and sympathy.

We have written this page to assist you with accepted customs and some suggestions on how one can be of comfort to the bereaved.

Some of the most frequently asked questions about funeral etiquette are about the service, the ashes, the dress, the religion, whether children should attend, floral arrangements and more.

You will find quick-links to all of these at the end of this page.

We have tried to address everything we could think of, however, if there is something in particular you wish us to add, please e-mail us your suggestions via our "Contact Us" page and we will include it either on our web site or if appropriate in our Rage Page.

The Funeral - should you attend?

Someone asked us, "Should I attend my ex-husband's father's funeral?"

Our reply was: The main purpose of having a funeral (other than to bury the body) is for people to express their love and respect to the deceased and to get some personal closure and healing.

Only you know how much you cared for your ex-father-in-law.

Also, you need to consider your ex-husband's feelings at this sad time, if you are on good terms and your presence is not going to upset any members of his family, then by all means attend the funeral.

Visiting the bereaved - should you visit immediately or wait for an invitation?

Not only is it good funeral etiquette but it is common courtesy and caring to call on the bereaved to offer sympathy and help.

Usually about 15 minutes is sufficient time to express your sympathy.

However, if they are overwhelmed with grief or visitors, make it a short visit, if you know them well, take over the tea making and handling of the guests and ease the burden of having to cope with grief and visitors at the same time.

What should I say?

Words from the heart are more important than trying to use words from a book on funeral etiquette.

So using your own words, express your sympathy. Kind words about the deceased loved one are always appropriate. To help you prepare, you can think about any good memories or experiences you had with the deceased, or even write your own about the person that you know the family would like to hear.

There are some eulogy examples available online that might help you, so even if you aren't going to be speaking at the service, writing a eulogy can be a beneficial way to put your thoughts into order.

Family and loved ones usually just need to talk and express their feelings. Let them talk as much as they need without asking too many questions.

They are not necessarily looking for a response from you. They are trying to understand what has happened and in their own way come to terms with the fact their loved one has gone.

Just be there for them and if they are the type who usually embrace or kiss when greeting, a warm hug will be appreciated.

Phoning - is it appropriate to phone the family?

It is good etiquette to phone the family as soon as possible to offer your sympathy. Try to keep the call brief as others will probably be trying to call as well.

Also, the family will more than likely be busy with visitors and funeral arrangements.

Funeral Etiquette and E-mailing - is it appropriate to send an e-mail offering condolences?

Condolences via e-mail are appropriate only if you are not a close friend or relative of the family.

But generally speaking, it is not good funeral etiquette to send an email, a hand written note or card would be more appropriate.

Private Funeral - what is it? Would it be a breach of funeral etiquette to attend without an invitation?

A private funeral service is one that is closed to the public.

Attendance is by invitation only. So unless you received a request from the family please do not attend, it would be considered intrusive and bad etiquette.

However, you could phone the family and offer condolences or send a card or flowers.

Food for the bereaved family

During the days immediately following the death the family is usually too overwhelmed to carry on the normal everyday living chores, such as cooking and cleaning. So food would be more than welcome.

But, before just bringing containers of food, check with the family to see what other people are bringing.

I have had the experience of having so many containers of soup and pasta that I had absolutely no space in the refrigerator or freezer to keep it all.

Also, I had no idea of which dish belonged to whom.

Some people also make a cash donation to families who have suffered a loss to help them cover the cost of the services. Funeral Etiquette for the after-funeral gathering

Immediately after the funeral, the family sometimes invites the attendees to join them for food or a reception at their home or designated place.

This gives everyone a chance to talk and provides some time to relax and refresh.

Sometimes friends or church members will take it upon themselves to prepare food ahead of time for this gathering to relieve the family of this task.

25 Life Lessons from Albert Einstein

1. Intellectual growth should commence at birth and cease only at death.

2. Everyone should be respected as an individual, but no one idolized.

3. Never do anything against conscience even if the state demands it.

4. If people are good only because they fear punishment, and hope for reward, then we are a sorry lot indeed.

5. A perfection of means, and confusion of aims, seems to be our main problem.

6. *Love is a better teacher than duty.*

7. *If you can't explain it simply, you don't understand it well enough.*

8. *No problem can be solved from the same level of consciousness that created it.*

9. *Insanity: doing the same thing over and over again and expecting different results.*

10. *Learn from yesterday, live for today, hope for tomorrow.*

11. *It has become appallingly obvious that our technology has exceeded our humanity.*

12. Everything that can be counted does not necessarily count; everything that counts cannot necessarily be counted.

13. Force always attracts men of low morality.

14. Everything should be as simple as it is, but not simpler.

15. A man should look for what is, and not for what he thinks should be.

16. Any man who reads too much and uses his own brain too little falls into lazy habits of thinking.

17. A person who never made a mistake never tried anything new.

18. It is the supreme art of the teacher to awaken joy in creative expression and knowledge.

19. Anyone who doesn't take truth seriously in small matters cannot be trusted in large ones either.

20. Great spirits have always encountered violent opposition from mediocre minds.

21. Education is what remains after one has forgotten what one has learned in school.

22. Logic will get you from A to B. Imagination will take you everywhere.

23. Anger dwells only in the bosom of fools.

24. Information is not knowledge.

25. Never lose a holy curiosity.

HILL'S HABITS OF PEOPLE WHO ARE SO LIKABLE THAT OTHERS GO OUT OF THEIR WAY TO HELP THEM

1. They develop a positive mental attitude and let it be seen and felt by others.

It's often easier to give into pessimism, but those who choose to be positive set themselves up for success and have better reputations.

2. They always speak in a carefully disciplined, friendly tone.

The best communicators speak deliberately and confidently, which gives their voice a pleasing sound.

3. They pay close attention to someone speaking to them.

Using a conversation as an opportunity to lecture someone "may feed the ego, but it never attracts people or makes friends," Hill says.

4. They are able to maintain their composure in all circumstances.

An overreaction to something either positive or negative can give people a poor impression. In the latter case, says Hill, "Remember that silence may be much more effective than your angry words."

5. They are patient.

"Remember that proper timing of your words and acts may give you a big advantage over impatient people," Hill writes.

6. They keep an open mind.

Those who close themselves off from certain ideas and associate only with like-minded people are missing out on not only personal growth but also opportunities for advancing their careers.

7. They smile when speaking with others.

Hill says that President Franklin D. Roosevelt's greatest asset was his "million-dollar smile," which allowed people to lower their guards during conversation.

8. They know that not all their thoughts need to be expressed.

The most likable people know that it's not worth offending people by expressing all their thoughts, even if they happen to be true.

9. They don't procrastinate.

Procrastination communicates to people that you're afraid of taking action, Hill says, and are therefore ineffective.

10. They engage in at least one good deed a day.

The best networkers help other people out without expecting anything in return.

11. They find a lesson in failure rather than brood over it.

People admire those who grow from failure rather than wallow in it. "Express your gratitude for having gained a measure of wisdom, which would not have come without defeat," Hill says.

12. They act as if the person they are speaking to is the most important person in the world.

The most likable people use conversations as an opportunity to learn about another person and give them time to talk.

13. They praise others in a genuine way without being excessive.

"Praise the good traits of others, but don't rub it on where it is not deserved or spread it too thickly," Hill says.

14. They have someone they trust point out their flaws.

Successful people don't pretend to be likable; they are likable because they care about their conduct and reputation. Having a confidant who can be completely honest with them allows them to continue growing.

Gotz me manners, Olive. Now gives me my spinach.